Lerner SPORTS

SPORTS
ALL-ST★RS

TIGER WOODS

Jon M. Fishman

Lerner Publications ◆ Minneapolis

Copyright © 2020 by Lerner Publishing Group, Inc.

All rights reserved. International copyright secured. No part of this book may be reproduced, stored in a retrieval system, or transmitted in any form or by any means—electronic, mechanical, photocopying, recording, or otherwise—without the prior written permission of Lerner Publishing Group, Inc., except for the inclusion of brief quotations in an acknowledged review.

Lerner Publications Company
An imprint of Lerner Publishing Group, Inc.
241 First Avenue North
Minneapolis, MN 55401 USA

For reading levels and more information, look up this title at www.lernerbooks.com.

Main body text set in Albany Std.
Typeface provided by Agfa.

Library of Congress Cataloging-in-Publication Data

Names: Fishman, Jon M., author.
Title: Tiger Woods / Jon M. Fishman.
Description: Minneapolis : Lerner Publications, [2020] | Series: Sports all-stars |
    Audience: Ages: 7–11. | Audience: Grades: K–3. | Includes bibliographical
    references and index.
Identifiers: LCCN 2019016950 (print) | LCCN 2019021888
    (ebook) | ISBN 9781541583610 (eb pdf) | ISBN 9781541577244 (lb : alk. paper) |
    ISBN 9781541589599 (pb : alk. paper)
Subjects: LCSH: Woods, Tiger—Juvenile literature. | Golfers—United States—
    Biography—Juvenile literature. | African American golfers—United States—
    Biography—Juvenile literature.
Classification: LCC GV964.W66 (ebook) | LCC GV964.W66 F57 2020 (print) | DDC
    796.352092 [B]—dc23

LC record available at https://lccn.loc.gov/2019016950

Manufactured in the United States of America
1-46746-47737-9/9/2019

CONTENTS

MASTERS CHAMPION

Woods always wears red on the final day of tournaments.

Tiger Woods gripped his golf club at the 2019 Masters Tournament. He stood on the **green** at the 12th hole and stared at his ball. It was only about 4 feet (1.2 m) from the hole. He stepped forward and took two relaxed practice swings. Then he adjusted his feet and swung at the ball.

- **Date of Birth:** December 30, 1975

- **Position:** golfer

- **League: PGA Tour**

- **Professional Highlights:** became the youngest golfer ever to win the Masters in 2001; was the first golfer to hold the titles of all four major tournaments at the same time; won the Masters for the fifth time in 2019

- **Personal Highlights:** became a famous golfer at the age of two; had spinal fusion surgery in 2017, solving years of back pain; helps thousands of young students reach their dreams through education

At first, the huge **gallery** was silent. People began to cheer as the ball rolled toward the hole. The cheers swelled to a roar as it dropped in. Woods raised his hand to the gallery as the fans shouted and clapped.

Woods had just tied Francesco Molinari for the lead on the final day of the tournament. The Masters is one of the **majors**, golf's four most important tournaments. Woods had won the Masters four times before. But he hadn't won the event since 2005. In recent years, injuries had prevented him from winning any PGA Tour event.

Woods made **birdies** on three of the final six holes. He finished the tournament 13 strokes below **par**, one

The crowd goes wild for Woods's fifth Masters win in 2019.

Woods has often ranked as the best golfer in the world. Since his first pro season in 1996, the Official World Golf Ranking has listed Woods number one for a total of 683 weeks. That equals more than 13 years! In 2019, Woods ranked fifth in the world.

stroke ahead of three other golfers. He had won the Masters again!

After taking his final shot, Woods pumped his fist. He threw both arms into the air and shouted with joy to the cheering gallery. Then he looked for his son, Charlie. Woods hugged the 10-year-old boy and lifted him off his feet. The moment reminded fans of 1997, the first time Woods won the Masters. That year he shared a hug with his father, Earl Woods, after taking his final shot.

The victory in 2019 was the 15th major title for Woods. He trails retired golfer Jack Nicklaus by three on the all-time list of wins in a major tournament. But the day of the 2019 Masters, more people were talking about Woods's incredible performance than his place in history. "I think this is one of the best sports stories we've ever seen," said former Masters champion Trevor Immelman.

TIGER'S TIME

Fourteen-year-old Tiger with his parents, Earl and Kultida

Tiger's father, Earl Woods, served in the US Army during the Vietnam War (1957–1975).

While in Vietnam, Woods became friends with a Vietnamese soldier.

Woods and his father (*center*) had a close relationship, and Woods credits him with his success in golf.

Woods gave his friend the nickname Tiger. When his son was born, Woods decided to call him Tiger too, after his friend. Eldrick "Tiger" Woods was born on December 30, 1975, in Cypress, California.

Earl Woods had been playing golf for about a year when Tiger was born. Young Tiger watched his father practice hitting balls into a net. Tiger was just six months old when he first tried to copy Earl's golf swing. Just like that, he was hooked on the sport.

Tiger loved golf partly because he was incredibly good at it. With his father as his coach, Tiger quickly became famous. When he was two, he played golf on TV for the first time, showing off his skills to a talk show host. People couldn't believe that such a young kid could play so well. He appeared on TV many times to show off his golf skills in the years ahead.

Tiger and his father hold Tiger's trophy from the 1991 US Junior Amateur.

By 1991, Tiger was one of the top **amateur** players in the United States. That year he played in the United States Golf Association (USGA) Junior Amateur Championship, or the US Junior Amateur. The tournament is for the best US amateur players under the age of 19. At 15, Tiger was younger than many of the other players. Yet he beat them all to win the tournament. He was the youngest golfer to become champion in the event's 43-year history.

Woods in 1996, after winning the first tournament of his pro career

The victory was the beginning of an incredible winning streak. Tiger won the next two US Junior Amateurs. He's the only golfer to win the tournament three years in a row.

The US Amateur is a tournament for amateur players of any age. Unlike the junior tournament, it is mostly for older, more experienced golfers. Beginning in 1994, Woods won the US Amateur three years in a row. He was more than ready to take on the world's top players on the PGA Tour.

Woods's first tournament as a pro was the 1996 Greater Milwaukee Open. He tied for 60th place. About one month later, he won his first PGA Tour event. He beat Davis Love III in a **playoff** to win the Las Vegas Invitational. By spring 1997, he ranked number one in the world.

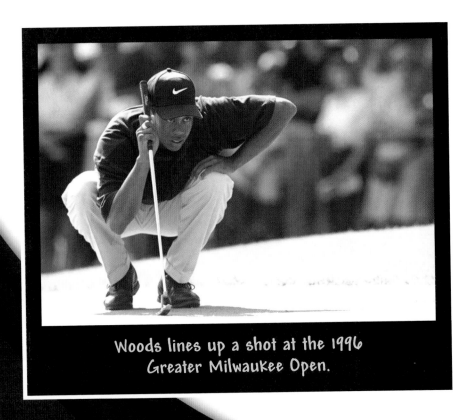

Woods lines up a shot at the 1996 Greater Milwaukee Open.

"A WALKING MIRACLE"

Before Woods made his mark on the sport, golfers didn't tend to focus on training their bodies.

Woods has been training to improve his golf game since he was six months old. In his first years as a pro, Woods trained harder than any golfer in the world.

Every morning, Woods ran 4 miles (6.4 km). Then he'd go to the gym to lift weights and build muscle. Next was the **driving range**. He would hit golf balls for up to three hours. He followed that with a round of golf and a practice session to focus on short shots. Another 4-mile run and a game of tennis or basketball ended the day's training.

Woods always spends time warming up before he competes in a tournament.

Such intense workouts can be hard on a person's body. Woods has had many injuries. Sometimes he tried to return to golf too quickly after hurting himself. If an injury isn't healed, it can be reinjured more easily.

Woods first had knee surgery in 1994 to remove benign, or noncancerous, tumors. He's had a series of knee and leg problems since then. In 2010, he withdrew from a tournament because of back pain. He later had four surgeries on his back.

In 2017, Woods had spinal fusion surgery. This type of surgery permanently connects two or more bones in a person's back. It helped relieve pain in Woods's back and leg.

After surgery, an X-ray of
Woods's back would have
shown the two bottom
bones joined together.

Another surgery in 2017 finally helped relieve his back pain. As he recovered, Woods slowly rebuilt the strength his body had lost from the surgery and other injuries.

To keep his body healthy, Woods doesn't work out as much as he once did. He knows that many people wouldn't be able to golf after suffering similar injuries. Yet he isn't just golfing—he's winning tournaments at the world's highest level. Modern medicine and hard work have done wonders for Woods. "I'm a walking miracle," he said.

Woods wears his fifth green Masters jacket after winning the tournament in 2019.

Woods began to work with Nike early in his career.

Woods speaks to reporters in 1996.

In 1996, Tiger Woods was ready to take the golf world by storm and join the PGA Tour.

But he needed to borrow money first.

Companies such as Nike partner with athletes to showcase their products.

Butch Harmon had been coaching Woods since 1993. Harmon told Woods that the entry fee for the 1996 Greater Milwaukee Open was $100. "Butch, I don't have one hundred dollars," Woods said. Harmon agreed to cover the fee. It was the last time in his life that Woods would have to worry about money.

Earlier that year, Woods had agreed to **endorse** Nike. He didn't have the money yet, but the company would pay him about $40 million to help bring attention to the brand. Nike announced the deal by airing a commercial on TV.

The "Hello, World" commercial showed Woods golfing at different ages and talked about how he had become one of the world's best golfers. The ad said that Woods still couldn't play at some golf courses because of the color of his skin. In the 1990s, some private golf courses in the United States barred black people from playing. The ad called attention to racism in the United States and made Woods a household name.

Woods's Nike deal was just the beginning. He has endorsed many products, from watches to energy drinks to tires. He's earned about $1.4 billion in his career. Of that huge total, less than 10 percent is from golf winnings.

Woods won $486,000 at his first Masters in 1997.

Woods's children often come to tournaments to support him.

Woods lives the life of a superrich athlete. He built a home in Jupiter, Florida, for $55 million. The huge property has its own small golf course. His yacht, *Privacy*, is 155 feet (47 m) long. Woods travels around the world to see pro tennis matches and other sporting events. He loves to spearfish. He also spends a lot of time with his daughter, Sam, and son, Charlie.

The year he became a pro golfer, Woods started TGR Foundation, A Tiger Woods Charity. TGR works to help students build confidence and prepare them for the future. The group's message is that young people can follow their dreams through education.

TGR has many programs to help students. The group provides science, technology, engineering, and math (STEM) education and starts students on STEM career paths. It gives young people money to attend college. TGR has affected the lives of tens of thousands of students. Woods wants to do even more. "We are just getting started," he said.

Woods speaks at a TGR Foundation event in 2016.

MAJOR
WINNER

Woods won the 1997 Masters by 12 shots, finishing with a score of 18 below par.

Woods secured his place as a sports megastar at the 1997 Masters. He won with the best score in the famous golf tournament's history. He was the youngest champion ever and the first person with African heritage to win the tournament.

After the 1997 Masters, some golfers predicted Woods would win 10 or even 20 more. He won his second in 2001.

Woods plays his best golf in the sport's four most important tournaments, known as the majors. He has won the Masters five times and the PGA Championship four times. He's taken first place at the US Open and the British Open three times each. In 2001, he became the first golfer to hold the titles of all four majors at once. In 2019, his fifth Masters win brought him to 15 wins across the majors, the second most in golf history.

Few athletes have changed their sport as much as Woods has changed golf. He inspired a generation of golfers to take fitness more seriously. His popularity drew millions of new fans to the sport, and the number of TV viewers watching golf soared. With more money coming into golf, players began winning bigger prizes at PGA Tour events.

Over his more than 20-year career, Woods has made his name as one of the greatest golfers of all time.

Woods has already changed golf forever, but he isn't finished yet. He continues to push himself, and he continues to win. With his historic talent and fierce desire to succeed, Woods has more victories in his future.

Woods watches a shot in May 2019.

All-Star Stats

People have different opinions about the greatest golfers of all time. But most fans agree that the best golfers win the most important events. When Tiger Woods won the 2019 Masters, he proved again that no active golfer matches his ability to win majors. Where will he rank on the all-time Masters win list when he retires?

Golfer	All-Time Masters Tournament Wins
Jack Nicklaus	6
Tiger Woods	**5**
Arnold Palmer	4
Gary Player	3
Jimmy Demaret	3
Nick Faldo	3
Phil Mickelson	3
Sam Snead	3

Source Notes

7   Bob Harig, "He's Back: Tiger Wins First Masters since 2005," ESPN, April 15, 2019, http://www.espn .com/golf/story/_/id/26524165/back-tiger-wins-first -masters-2005.

17 Lawrence Ostlere, "'A Walking Miracle': How Tiger Woods Came Back to Be in Masters Contention Happy, Healthy and with a New Swing," *Independent* (London), April 5, 2018, https://www.independent .co.uk/sport/golf/tiger-woods-masters-2018-augusta -comeback-spinal-fusion-surgery-a8289311.html.

20 John Strege, "Tiger Woods' Professional Debut: Ten Things You Might Not Have Known or Remembered," *Golf Digest*, August 29, 2016, https://www.golfdigest .com/story/tiger-woods-professional-debut-ten-things -you-might-not-have-known-or-remembered.

23 Tiger Woods, "A Message from Tiger," TGR Foundation, A Tiger Woods Charity, accessed February 17, 2019, https://tgrfoundation.org/about/.

amateur: a person who takes part in an unpaid activity

birdies: scores of one less than par on a hole

driving range: a place to practice hitting golf balls

endorse: to show public support for something, usually to help sell it

gallery: fans at a golf match

green: a smooth, grassy area containing a hole on a golf course

majors: golf's four most important tournaments. The majors include the Masters, the PGA Championship, the US Open, and the British Open.

par: a score that equals the standard number of strokes needed for a hole

PGA Tour: the top level of pro golf in the United States

playoff: holes played to decide a winner if two or more golfers are tied with the best score after the final hole of a tournament

pro: a person who does a job or plays a sport for money

Braun, Eric. *Incredible Sports Trivia: Fun Facts and Quizzes.* Minneapolis: Lerner Publications, 2018.

Glave, Tom. *Tiger Woods vs. Jack Nicklaus.* Minneapolis: SportsZone, 2018.

Golf Facts for Kids
https://wiki.kidzsearch.com/wiki/Golf

Junior Golf—PGA.com
https://www.pga.com/pga-america/juniors

Lemke, Christina. *Golf.* Vero Beach, FL: Rourke, 2016.

Tiger Woods
https://tigerwoods.com/

Index

Photo Acknowledgments

Image credits: David Cannon/Getty Images, p. 4; Andrew Redington/Getty Images, p. 6; Ken Levine/Getty Images, p. 8; J.D. Cuban/Allsport/Getty Images, pp. 9, 11, 12; Rick Dole/Getty Images, p. 10; Mike Ehrmann/Getty Images, pp. 13, 14, 17; Callista Images/Getty Images, p. 16; Donald Miralle/Getty Images, p. 18; Mark Perlstein/The LIFE Images Collection/Getty Images, p. 19; Andrew Redington/Getty Images, p. 20; Augusta National/Getty Images, pp. 21, 24, 25, 26; ANDREW CABALLERO-REYNOLDS/AFP/Getty Images, p. 22; RMhoto by Lester Cohen/Getty Images, p. 23; David Cannon/Getty Images, p. 27.

Cover Image: Kyodo News/Getty Images.